HANDBOOK
FOR
GRADE ONE
CERTIFICATE EXAMINATION
IN
ELECTRIC
GUITAR
PLAYING

This handbook was compiled by
Tony Skinner
on behalf of
The Registry of Electric Guitar Tutors
Honorary Patrons

Hank Marvin, Rory Gallagher, Ivor Mairants, Paul Samson
John Etheridge, Mick Green, Dave Kelly, Glenn Tilbrook

British Library Cataloguing in Publication Data

Skinner, Tony
London College of Music Handbook for
Certificate Examinations in Electric
Guitar Playing - Grade One
I. Title
787.87076

ISBN 1-898466-01-7

Published in Great Britain by

*The Registry
of
Electric Guitar Tutors*

Printing and typesetting by

Take Note
Publishing Limited

97 Buckland Way, Worcester Park, Surrey KT4 8NR

CONTENTS

FOREWORD

By the Director of Examinations at The London College of Music

The London College of Music was founded in 1887 as an establishment devoted to musical education. Local examinations were organised at the same time, and now the London College of Music, based at Thames Valley University, is one of the four leading boards offering recognised examinations in a wide range of musical subjects throughout the United Kingdom and overseas.

In 1960 the London College of Music was one of the first examination boards in the United Kingdom to introduce graded examinations for classical guitar. Over the last 30 years the electric guitar has come to play a fundamental role in the development of most styles of popular music. With the increasing acknowledgement of popular music as an area worthy of serious study, the London College of Music is again at the forefront with the establishment of a specialist and comprehensive range of fully validated examinations in electric guitar playing. These may prove in time to be seen as a landmark in popular music education.

The examinations provide hitherto unavailable recognition and validation of the skills and talents of electric guitar players, and may help both students and teachers of the electric guitar to become integrated into the mainstream of music education.

The accompanying series of Examination Handbooks provide an unrivalled comprehensive source of theoretical knowledge and practical insight into the electric guitar. They serve as a structured and essential study aid for any candidates working towards the London College of Music examinations. Each Handbook covers all the material required for each examination grade, giving clear examples of the requirements and standard. The Handbooks provide a solid foundation of musical education for the electric guitarist.

Martyn Williams B.Mus(Dunelm) G.R.S.M. F.R.C.O. F.L.C.M. A.R.C.M. M.T.C.(London) Hon. L.C.M.

INTRODUCTION

This Handbook is primarily intended to give advice and information to candidates considering taking the Grade One Examination in Electric Guitar Playing, although undoubtedly it will be found that the information contained within will be helpful to all guitarists whether intending to take the examination or not.

The prime aim of this Handbook is to aid the establishment of good musical and technical foundations. Whilst this handbook can be used for independent study it is ideally intended as a supplement to individual or group tuition, and is not designed to replace the need for guitar tuition from an experienced tutor.

In order that the information in regard to scales and chords can be illustrated as clearly as possible and made available for all to understand regardless of experience, the relevant notation and fingering is displayed via the use of the GUITAROGRAPH.

GUITAROGRAPH

The GUITAROGRAPH uses a combination of tablature, traditional notation and fingerboard diagram. These are explained individually below:

(1) TABLATURE

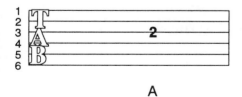

A

The horizontal lines represent the strings in descending order as indicated, whilst the numbers on the string lines refer to the frets at which the left hand fingers should press.

Example shown ➤ Play at the second fret on the third string.

(2) TREBLE CLEF NOTATION

The lines and spaces of the treble clef indicate notes as follows :

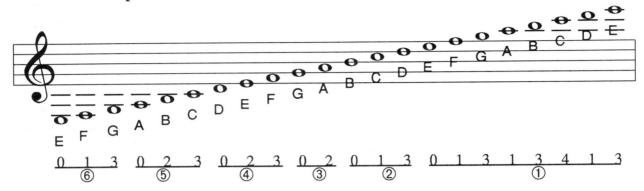

A sharp (#) before a note would raise its pitch by a semitone i.e. one fret higher, whilst a flat (♭) before a note would lower the pitch by a semitone, i.e. one fret lower.

In the illustration, above the lower circled numbers refer to the string on which each note could be played, whilst the number immediately below each note indicates which left hand finger could be used. The fingering in the above illustration is shown only to illustrate the exact pitch of each note.

Example shown ➤ play the note of A at the pitch shown.

(3) FINGERBOARD DIAGRAM

Each horizontal line represents a single string. The vertical lines represent the frets – the numbers of which are indicated above them in Roman Numerals. The numbers within the diagram indicate the left hand finger to be used.

Example Shown ➤ play on the 2nd fret of the G string using the 2nd finger.

GUITAROGRAPH

All the three methods above are ways of illustrating the same information and within this Handbook a combination of all methods is used via the means of the GUITAROGRAPH, thereby ensuring clarity and leaving no doubt as to what is required.

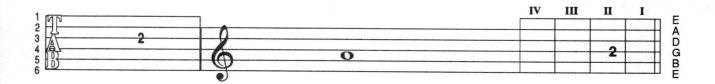

In the example shown above all three notations refer to the same note, i.e. A on the 2nd fret of the 3rd (G) string using the 2nd finger.

INTERVAL FORMULAE

Above each Guitarograph diagram is a scale or chord formula. This lists the letter names of the notes within the scale or chord, together with their interval numbers. The interval numbers shown are based on their comparison to the major scale of the same root thus aiding comparative analysis. Example :

C Major chord			C Minor chord		
C	E	G	C	E♭	G
R	3	5	R	♭3	5

ALTERNATIVE FINGERING

When using the GUITAROGRAPHS please remember that whilst the notes indicated are precise and definitive, the left hand fingering given in all cases is only one possible recommended suggestion, and any alternative systematic and effective fingerings devised by your tutor or yourself may be acceptable.

TUNING

For grades up to and including Grade 3 it is not necessarily expected that candidates will be able to accurately tune their own guitars, and consequently the examiner can provide assistance in this matter if requested.

The use of electronic tuners, tuning forks, pitch pipes or other tuning aids prior to or at the start of the examination is permitted, but candidates should be able to make any further adjustments as required during the examination unaided. The examiner will upon request offer an E or A note to tune to.

For examination purposes guitars should be tuned to Standard Concert Pitch, i.e. A=440Hz, which means E=329.6Hz.

Candidates who normally tune to non-standard pitch e.g. A=442Hz et al. should revert to Standard Concert Pitch for examination purposes. Candidates who tune a full tone or semitone higher / lower should either revert to Standard Pitch for the examination or should be prepared to transpose immediately upon request all requirements to Standard Pitch.

SECTION 1 - SCALES

Below are illustrated the scales required for the
Grade I Examination :

E NATURAL MINOR - 2 OCTAVES

E	F#	G	A	B	C	D	E
R	2	♭3	4	5	♭6	♭7	R

E BLUES - 2 OCTAVES

E	G	A	A#	B	D	E
R	♭3	4	#4	5	♭7	R

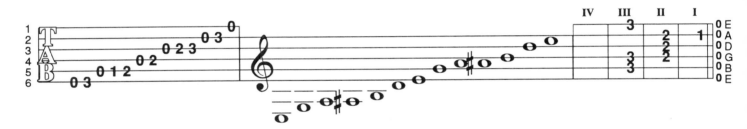

G PENTATONIC MAJOR - 2 OCTAVES

G	A	B	D	E	G
R	2	3	5	6	R

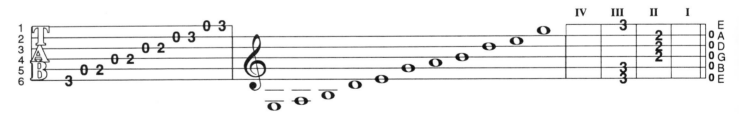

A MAJOR - 2 OCTAVES

A	B	C#	D	E	F#	G#	A
R	2	3	4	5	6	7	R

A PENTATONIC MINOR - 2 OCTAVES

A	C	D	E	G	A
R	♭3	4	5	♭7	R

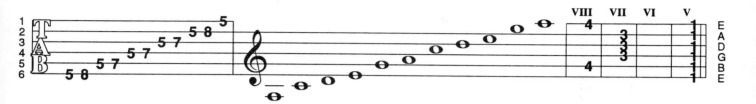

GENERAL INFORMATION AND ADVICE IN REGARD TO SCALE PLAYING

The examiner may request you to play any of the above scales. Each scale should be played once only ascending and descending, i.e. from the lowest note to the highest and back again without a pause and without repeating the top note.

Choose a tempo at which you feel confident and comfortable and try to maintain this evenly throughout – evenness and clarity are more important than speed for its own sake.

LEFT-HAND TECHNIQUE

Press the tips of the left-hand fingers as close to the frets as possible. This minimises both buzzes and the amount of pressure required, enabling you to play with a lighter, clearer and hence more fluent touch.

Try to keep all the left-hand fingers close to the fingerboard and have them ready to press in a hovering position as this minimises the amount of movement required. Always have the left hand spread with the fingers correctly spaced and ready in position hovering before you start to play.

RIGHT-HAND TECHNIQUE

Whilst it is not essential to use a plectrum for this examination, you may find that the use of the fingers or nails has a detrimental influence on speed, attack, volume and tone – or at least more effort will be required to achieve the same effect. On the other hand the use of the fingers rather than the plectrum does offer greater flexibility, particularly harmonically, for example in the facility of playing two or more notes simultaneously on non-adjacent strings. Ultimately the choice is personal, but a fluency in both methods is perhaps the most desirable resolution.

If using a plectrum ensure to always alternate downstrokes with upstrokes. Grip the pick between the index finger and thumb. Position the pick so that its point is about a quarter of an inch beyond the fingertip. If an excessive amount of plectrum tip extends beyond the finger a lack of pick control will result as the plectrum will flap around when striking the strings – this would consequently reduce fluency and accuracy.

Be careful not to grip the plectrum too tightly as excessive gripping pressure can lead to muscular tension in the right hand with subsequent loss of flexibility and movement. Avoid holding the pick so that its tip is at right angles to the index finger as this will severely limit the freedom of the right-hand wrist and thereby encourage excessive right arm movement.

Try not to rest the fingers of the right hand on the body of the guitar since this restricts freedom of movement in the right hand and wrist. It also prevents the plectrum maintaining the same angle as it picks across the strings.

SECTION 2 - CHORDS

This Handbook and examination use the standard abbreviations of an upper case letter with a '7' to refer to a dominant seventh chord, whilst a lone upper case letter refers to a major chord, a lower case 'm' after a letter name refers to a minor chord and Maj7 refers to a major 7th chord. For Example:

D = D Major	D7 = D Dominant 7th	Dm = D Minor	D Maj7 = D Major 7th

Major chords

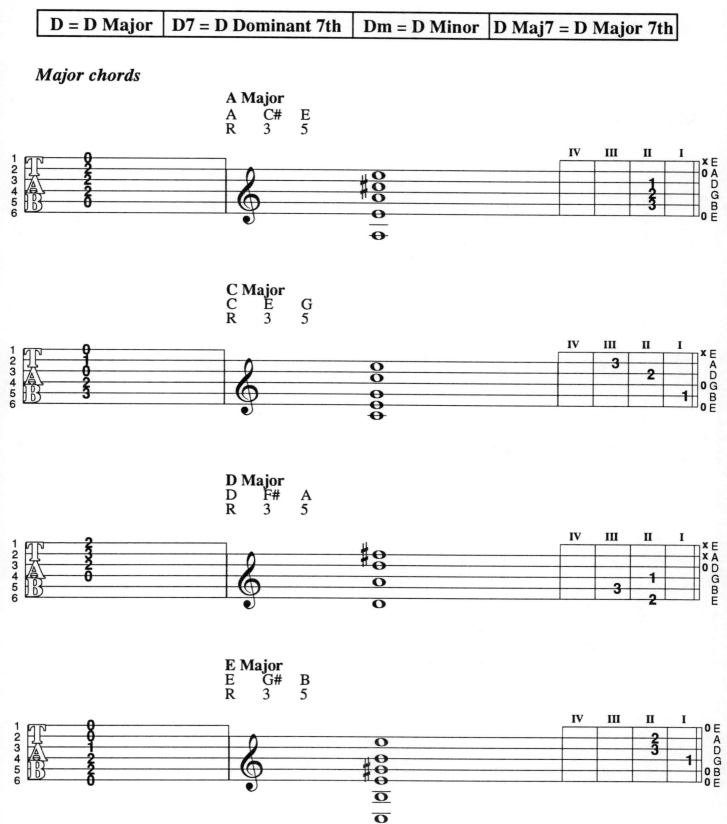

11

G Major

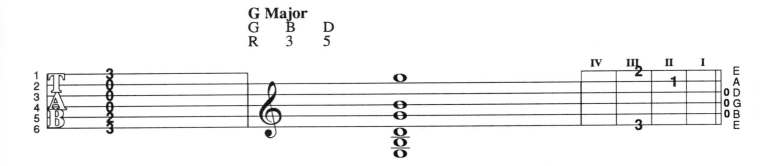

Minor chords

A Minor

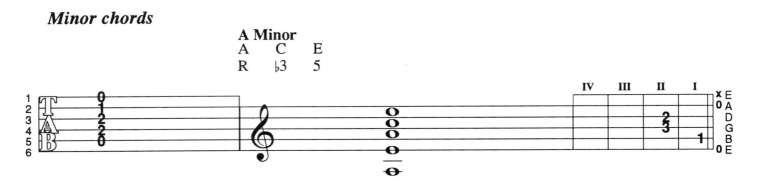

D Minor

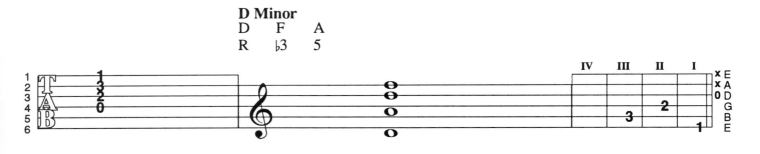

E Minor

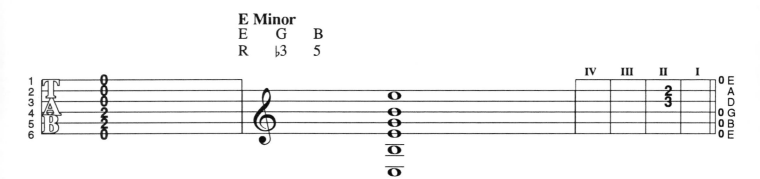

Dominant 7th chords

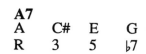

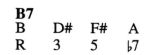

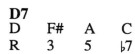

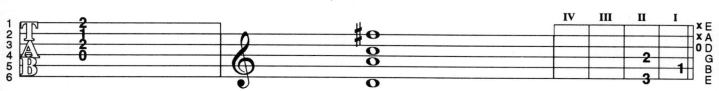

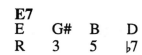

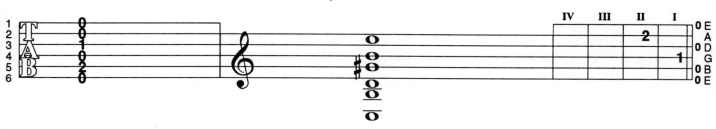

Major 7th chords

GENERAL INFORMATION & ADVICE IN REGARD TO CHORD PLAYING

The examiner may request you to play any of the above chords. Each chord should be played once only using a single downstroke. Make sure that your fingers are carefully and correctly positioned before playing the chord. Ensure that you use the tips of your left-hand fingers and that no required open strings are muted. Press as closely to the frets as possible to aid clarity and minimise fret buzz.

In the above diagrams strings which should be omitted are marked by an X, so be careful not to strike these strings when playing the chord.

14

SECTION 3 – RHYTHM PLAYING

Candidates will be given a chord chart and will be allowed a short time to study it before being asked to play it. The chord chart will contain only the chords listed in Section 2 of this Handbook. Some examples of the type of chart that may be presented at this grade are given below.

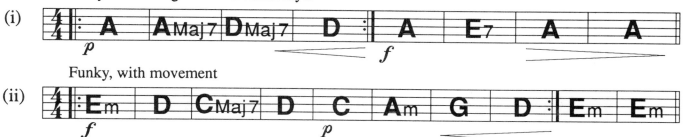

At this grade the time signature is limited to $\frac{4}{4}$ – i.e. 4 crotchet beats per bar, although this does not necessarily mean that candidates should restrict themselves to merely 4 strums per bar. The more imaginative the rhythmic playing of the candidate the higher the mark that may be achieved, as long as the time signature is evident by maintaining a regular pulse and the tempo is even, with no unnecessary slowing – particularly at bar lines.

It will aid fluency of rhythm playing if the strumming hand pivots from the wrist, a fluid and easy strumming action is best achieved this way, with the wrist loose and relaxed. If the wrist is stiff and not allowed to move freely then excessive arm movement will occur as the strumming action will be forced to come from the elbow instead. As this can never move as fluently as the wrist action there will be a loss of smoothness and rhythmic potential.

Marks will be awarded for accuracy of chords – so aside from ensuring that the left hand has fingered the correct frets and strings, candidates should also pay attention to the striking of strings with the right hand, for example be particularly careful not to strum the 6th string on B7 or on all D chords. Chord changes should be as smooth and fluid as possible and lack any sense of hesitation. Chords should ring clear, i.e. free of fret buzz or the unintended damping of notes with the left-hand fingers.

Be careful not to overgrip with the left-hand thumb on the back of the neck as this will cause muscle fatigue and tend to limit freedom of the thumb to move. It is essential that the left-hand thumb is allowed to move freely when changing chords. If the thumb remains static this restricts the optimum positioning of the fingers for the next chord which may result in unnecessary left hand stretching and the involuntary dampening of certain strings as the fingers are not positioned upright on their tips. Also be aware that for the left-hand thumb to move freely the wrist, elbow and shoulder must be flexible and relaxed, try to ensure that this is not inhibited by your standing or sitting position.

During the time given to look over the chord chart candidates should look for any markings of time signature and tempo that are given, and should particularly try to discover the overall structure of the sequence.

At this grade the only indications on the chart other than the time signature, tempo and style are repeat and dynamic markings. Passages to be repeated are indicated by two vertical dots at the start and end of the section to be repeated. For example :

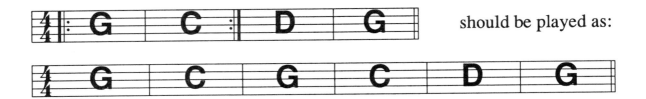 should be played as:

Dynamic markings are explained below :

p – play softly f – play strongly

     – become louder   – become softer

After playing the first chord sequence candidates may, at the examiner's discretion, be given an additional chart to play. This will be of a similar difficulty to the first one. Candidates should use this opportunity to display their range of rhythmic ability by performing the sequence in a different style.

SECTION 4 – LEAD PLAYING

The candidate will be shown a short chord sequence containing chords chosen from those listed in Section 2 of this handbook. The examiner will then play this sequence (either live or on tape) and the candidate should improvise over this using an appropriate scale selected from Section 1 of this handbook. Some examples are shown below:

(i) The scale of E Natural Minor could be used over the following sequence...

(ii) The scale of G Pentatonic Major could be used over the following sequence...

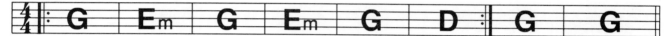

(iii) The scale of A Major could be used over the following sequence...

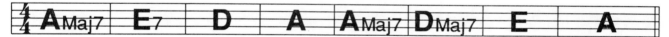

(iv) The scale of A Pentatonic Minor could be used over the following sequence...

The sequence will be played a total of three times – during the first playing the candidate should not play but rather listen and digest the sequence before improvising on the next two cycles, which will end on the tonic (i.e. first) chord.

Whilst candidates will need to select a scale to improvise from, they should be aware that the purpose of the scale is essentially to set the series of notes that will be in tune in a particular key and is not an end in itself. Thus candidates should endeavour to make their improvisation melodically and rhythmically inventive and imaginative rather than sounding scale-like.

The style of lead playing should enhance and empathize with the chordal accompaniment which may be from a range of musical styls such as rock, pop and blues. Candidates should try to create interesting melodic and rhythmic phrases within their improvisation and should avoid inappropriate use of continuous scalic playing. Playing should be fluent but without the need for speed for its own sake. More important is that there should be good co-ordination between both hands, with accurate left-hand fretting and sound right-hand plectrum / finger technique.

At the examiner's discretion an additional sequence may be selected for the candidate to improvise over. Although this will again contain chords only from Section 2 of this handbook, a contrasting tempo and style will be used and the candidate may need to select a different scale from Section 1 to improvise from. In such an instance candidates should ensure that the style of improvisation used reflects the nature of the chordal rhythm backing, and the improvisation should demonstrate a divergence from that previously presented thereby exhibiting the candidate's range and aptitude.

SECTION 5 – SPOKEN TESTS

In this section of the examination candidates will be asked questions about the scales which were used in Section 4, in particular they should be able to name any note from the required scales – so that when the examiner points to a particular string and fret the candidate should be able to name this note (which will be chosen from one of the required scales). In order to establish a solid musical foundation it is important that candidates should be aware of the notes that they are playing rather than merely duplicating finger patterns.

Candidates may also be asked questions about the correct positioning of the left-hand fingers and how to obtain clear notes and avoid fret buzz. As described in Section 1 of this handbook – the most important aspect is, whilst using the tips rather than the pads of the fingers, to spread the left hand so as one can press at the very edge of the frets.

Candidates may also be asked questions about right-hand technique. Here candidates should be aware of the advantages of keeping the right hand free from holding the guitar in place. It is not only unnecessary, but also restricting, to rest any fingers on the guitar body. If a plectrum is used, care should be taken to have an appropriate amount of plectrum tip protruding from the grip with index finger and thumb. Whilst this will vary with the size of one's fingers and the plectrum used, in general too much plectrum showing will drag or even snag on the strings thus hampering fluency and articulation, whilst too little increases the chances of missing the correct string altogether. Plectrum strokes should alternate between down and up strokes to facilitate fluency and speed.

Candidates should also have a basic general knowledge of the instrument. In particular:

(i)   Basic ways in which tone can be varied, such as changing the right-hand position, or for instance selecting the bridge pick-up for increased treble.

(ii) The function of the machine heads :

These are normally positioned by the headstock of the guitar. Each string has its own machine head (or turning head) which when rotated increases or reduces the tension exerted on that string, thereby raising or lowering its pitch. By carefully adjusting all of these the guitar can be brought into tune.

(iii) The meaning of common guitar terms such as :

Action – the distance between the strings and the frets, which determines the ease of fretting notes.

Marker dots – the dots or blocks inlaid into front and / or side of the fingerboard to act as a reminder as to the position of certain frets. These normally include at least frets 3, 5, 7, 9 & 12.

SECTION 6 – AURAL ASSESSMENTS

Part (a)

The examiner will twice tap (or play on a single note) a 2 bar rhythm in $\frac{4}{4}$ time – containing only minims, crotchets, quavers or semiquavers. The candidate should then attempt to reproduce this rhythm by tapping or playing. Some examples of the type of rhythm are given below.

(i)   (ii)

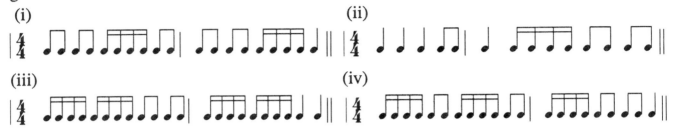

(iii)   (iv)

Part (b)

The candidate will be asked to look away whilst the examiner plays a 4 beat phrase. This will consist of adjacent notes taken from a scale listed in Section 1 of this handbook – the candidate will be told which scale is to be used, and the root note will be played. The phrase may consist of crotchets, quavers and semiquavers, with semiquavers only occurring on notes of the same pitch. The examiner will play the phrase twice before the candidate makes a first attempt to reproduce the phrase on the guitar. If required, the examiner will play the phrase one further time prior to the candidate's second attempt. Some examples of the type of phrase are shown below.

Taken from G Pentatonic Major Scale

Part (c)

The examiner will play a 4 bar phrase in $\frac{4}{4}$ time using only minims, crotchets , quavers and semiquavers. During the second playing the candidate should tap / clap the main pulse, accenting the first beat of each bar. An example is given below.

Examiner plays:

Candidate taps:

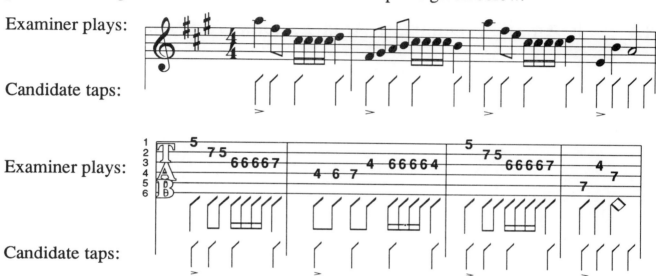

Examiner plays:

Candidate taps:

Part (d)

The examiner will play the note A followed by another note taken from the first five degrees of the A Major Scale. The candidate will then be asked to identify the second note both by letter name and interval number.

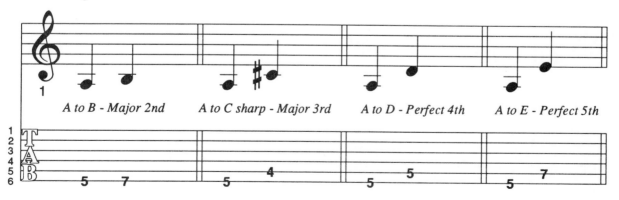

A to B - Major 2nd   A to C sharp - Major 3rd   A to D - Perfect 4th   A to E - Perfect 5th

It will be easier to remember the sound of these intervals if at first each one is related to the start of a familiar tune or riff. For example, the following traditional tunes start with a perfect fourth – Amazing Grace, Auld Lang Syne, Away in a Manger.

Part (e)

Whilst the candidate looks away, the examiner will play a few bars of music containing exclusively either major, minor, dominant 7th or major 7th chords. The candidate will then be asked which type of chords were used.

Examples :

(i)   ‖ A | D | A. D. | A ‖

(ii)   ‖ Am | Dm | Am. Dm. | Am ‖

(iii)   ‖ A7 | D7 | A7 . D7 . | A7 ‖

(iv)   ‖ Amaj7 | Dmaj7 | Amaj7 . Dmaj7 . | Amaj7 ‖

CONCLUSION

After having studied this handbook, if you wish to enter for the Certificate Examination please first ensure that you are familiar with the general regulations and requirements as shown in the current Examinations Syllabus.

An Examination Syllabus and entry form can be obtained by sending

an A5 sized S.A.E. to –

The Registry of Electric Guitar Tutors,

P.O. Box 873,

Purley,

Surrey CR8 2YG.